Author: Rishi Pal Sharma

People today are selfish and chance-passers. They do not express the truth in order to achieve their goal, but we need to consider this and understand how committed they are to us.

TRUST

Index

SHALL I TRUST?"

THE FIRST QUESTION WE ASK OURSELVES IS, "SHOULD I TRUST?" WHEN WE MEET A NEW PERSON, THE SECOND QUESTION IS HOW MUCH I SHOULD TRUST. HOW WOULD WE KNOW IF SOMEONE IS COMMITTED OR NOT? ALTERNATIVELY, CHECK THE LEVEL OF COMMITMENT.

Did these questions, do come in your mind.

If your answer is, yes! Then you need this book. With one time cost, you will learn the secret of committed. Once you know fundamental of committed secret, you can judge the person easily, who is nearby. You will understand the relationship level of committed or trust.

- ✓ How much of him or her, can you trust? Know the level of committed toward you.

People today are selfish and chance-passers. They do not express the truth in order to achieve their goal, but we need to consider this and understand how committed they are to us.

Can we trust every one of them?

Learn it once, and you can apply it forever. Give the connection more time to develop or end it right away. Simply check the degree or proportion of faith or trust before establishing a connection or attempting any transaction.

MAKE YOUR VISION CLEAR ABOUT WHO IS NEARBY.

- ✓ This allows for different perspectives on situations to be seen and understood.
- ✓ This allows us to recognize when interaction is required and to put in place mechanisms to protect one's own life as well as the lives of others.
- ✓ Perception begins with grasping another person's experience in order to understand his or her behavior.

I will cover all the aspects of the person, including whether you should trust a person or not. Have you ever thought, "Do we really need this? Yes, of course. An amazing fact will blow your mind. The best part is that once you know the secret, you can relax and have 99% faith in a person.

Nearby can be anybody; it may be a friend, relative, or colleague. Many people have surrounded us. However, we get confused about whom we should trust, whether we have approached or they have approached us. Connection in our lives plays a very important role. The people surround us all.

Peace, happiness, and satisfaction all come when we know that we are sitting with a person who will not ditch us.

Why is self-trust so important?

- When we do not accept ourselves as true enough, we lack a core reference point from which to operate.
- We may additionally lose our sense of ourselves, and glide consistent with others' agendas.
- We need to self-accept as true to the maximum while we are in conditions where we are unsure.
- We may be under the agency of people who are more influential than we are, or we may be under pressure because we need something.

For some reason or other, we are off-centre. If we know best, these are the instances when it is genuinely vital for our enterprise and our peace of mind that we consider ourselves.

In my opinion, if you are no longer aware of what you are doing or no longer capable of stopping yourself even while you realize you must, you cannot trust yourself. You are not in control. Whatever is in your thoughts or is in your control, no longer you.

INFLUENCED BY NEARBY

Our minds and behavior change because we have been influence by what is around us. It may be due to their position or power. Moreover, we do agree with their thoughts and we feel that they always think good for us. Again, you have to think. One thing you should be clear about is that you are the only person who can care for yourself. Therefore, this thought may help you gain more confidence in yourself. The best part is that when you start trusting yourself, you will always have a win-win situation.

PROVIDE FOR THE NEEDS OF OTHERS.

- ✓ You may gain a better understanding of how to engage the individual and respond in ways that meet both emotional needs and your objectives.
- ✓ People who are playful, extroverted, and open require stimulation and fun.
- ✓ They enjoy conversing and spending time with others.
- ✓ Give them your full attention and do things to keep it.
- ✓ With powerful, precise, or neurotic people, avoid small talk and get right to the point.
- ✓ Prepare to stand your ground with them or risk being run over.
- ✓ Understand that the disagreeable personality may create conflict or reasons why something will not work.
- ✓ Prepare for their objections.

However, we cannot live alone. Therefore, we need friends, relatives, and colleagues. We live in a society where selecting a person is a difficult task. So keep reading. I will share the secret of trust. In addition, once you know this, you will be on top.

Once you have a good team and companion. Nothing can be doing in the worst-case scenario. Confidence and good companions never let you down. So are you ready, to know more about the secret of trust.

Its gives you

- ✓ More confidence and more self-assurance
- ✓ Clear Vision of nearby person
- ✓ Understands involvement of his/her situation
- ✓ Understanding faith or trust, you can do.

For the disagreeable personality, understand that they may create conflict or reasons why something will not work.

Professionals who earn a high rating in this size experience developing and increasing their sphere of interpersonal impact. They take satisfaction in persuasion, negotiation, and the energy of maintaining precious data and ideas. This size of relational work is all about changing the factor of view or the behavior of others. An antique expression, "He may want to talk a canine off a meat truck," aptly describes high scorer's right here. Whether to a consumer or to a colleague whether they are ready to speak with me about a product, a carrier, or an idea—those human beings live to sell. Think of the manager to your company who is constantly capable of get more resources for his initiatives than everybody else is can. Alternatively, image that former boss of yours who could continually get humans fired up for the subsequent venture, irrespective of how tired they had been from the ultimate one.

At least once, in your existence someone will do something that makes you assert, "Why did they do this? How may want to they do this? I simply don't recognize." In fact, this could probably occur to you a number of times. You may additionally experience which you simply don't apprehend human beings – how they assume, the manner they act, or their reasons or intentions. But know-how people can help reduce warfare and improve your relationships. So take the time to evaluate their character, maintain an open mind, and apprehend yourself so that you can higher understand them.

Once you know that the faithful and committed person has surrounded you. Its gives you more pleasure and peace. Once you know the secret, of Trust, you always have win situation. In additional to this, you will understand the percentage of trust. How much you can trust it is 33%, 66% or more.

FRIENDSHIP BEGINS, WHEN HEART CONSIDERED AS SPECIAL TO SOMEONE.

Therefore, relationships journey begin with Heart.

Friendship for lots, to consist of scholarly people, is genuinely a few sorts of casual classes. Without specific boundaries like whilst you say a person is a chum, you do now, not say that he is your friend in school, or he's your pal inside the office, or a friend in any class of mission. Usually, friendship would indicate a mutual relationship which you supply and take for every different. Other, with a time span so that it will continually rely upon each celebration involved. The degree of friendship could commonly be dependent on the circumstances that ended in this type of dating. The degree of friendship with a classmate at school will be one of a kind than the diploma of friendship with a Neighbour Buddy. Even at paintings, the ties of friendship someone has along with his co-employees in an office will be one of a kind from the binds of friendship between squad dies. In maximum instances, the diploma of dependency among one another in a particular task would degree the degree of friendship amongst them.

Friendship makes many forms, like casual friends whom you could bear in mind already as friends, even when you have just met them as soon as, twice, or three instances in a gathering. Time friends, humans you have regarded because you had been younger, like your associates, and quality pals like your near buddies in businesses which you are continually with and who proportion with you anything they have, and you provide me something you've got in go back. These sharing among best friends are not most effective restrained to cloth matters but also would consist of religious and emotional sharing like retaining and advising your buddies to preserve up with their faith and different emotional troubles that they have got.

In sharing all factors of your everyday life, every now and then you operate friendship SMS textual content messages, lovable friendship texts so one can deepen the friendship among your companies of friends. There are, however, many folks that used friendship as a device for self-gains. The unhappy the aspect about these kinds of human beings would be the fact that once they have received their motive. Because of the friendship that they had been capable of establish, they just as all of sudden junk the pals.

That helped them within the first vicinity. These humans are those who are into consideration as friends for benefit women and people. There also are folks that will simplest make pals with individuals who proportion with them their passion. These human beings are those that we are able to categories as those who search for selective friendship. People on this category can be individuals who are into exclusive interests or undertakings that they cost so much that after they recognize you have the identical kind of aspiration would then try and recall you a pal in such a project. For example, someone a person with a ardor for horses can without problems make pals with someone inside the horse breeding business.

In addition, if you are a SCUBA enthusiast, you may make pals without difficulty with an underwater photographer.

After, you chanced to meet each other.

These styles of friendships are truly now not most effective related to hobbies like playing with your mobile telephone, sending SMS messages, sharing love texts, and different unique abilities that a person has to Make pals with other folks that share his interest in the identical discipline of undertaking. These can also be genuine to even bad behavior consisting of consuming, playing, and womanizing. This is precisely Why can we have this pronouncing? Tell me who your pals are, and I will inform you who you are.

The diploma of dependency among one another in a particular task would degree the degree of friendship amongst them.

Therefore, for me, the heart creates relationship. Moreover, starts bonding commitment or trust require the same feeling from the other side. Therefore, as per the friend's norms, all the things make you clear that 33% level of commitment.

PHYSICALLY APPEAR.

Yes, when a person starts giving time in every situation, he or she has entered the next level of a relationship. As per my experience, bad advice from anybody can ruin your life.

However, advice can be wrong, but when a friend or relative stands by you, there is a rare chance of receiving wrong advice or making the wrong decision. When a companion or buddy supports you and looks out for you in every circumstance, you can take your connection with him to the next level. Body language does convey a person's emotions.

Body language is a discipline about non-verbal behavior, one of the most powerful, personal and pretty language because it facilitates you understands emotions and feelings of people around you.

Body language is one of the most crucial languages to analyze because after you already know how to interpret the conduct of others you will realize what they sincerely suppose. Reading and interpreting frame language is an artwork and technological expertise. She makes each movement with a reason and it expresses something. Therefore, it may be very critical to find out studying frame language, alerts, smiles, gestures.

The artwork of interpreting body language is rarely a science. But, we do recognise some

basics that may help us read the emotions of others. A few examples comply with.

Crossed hands, as almost every salesclerk knows, way the man, or woman on the other facet of the Desk is protecting or now not receptive. On the alternative hand, if that man or woman leans ahead and maintains his or her eyes on you, then you definitely do have a receptive listener.

If you watch novice speakers, you may probable observe how they preserve their arms near their bodies, indicating a lack of self-belief. As they get extra practice speaking in public, you may see their arms move away from their aspects and become energetic equipment for conveying messages.

Arms wide open suggest consider and openness, as do open hands, while fingers held excessive above the head display a sense of victory, and clenched palms suggest anger.

Curiously, one of the maximum tough interpretations of frame language entails mendacity. Researchers have possibly spent more time on this issue of frame language than any other has. Moreover, their conclusions? The handiest surefire way to realize if another character is lying is to study very small and speedy wrinkling of the brow.

If you have not spent an awful lot time reading frame language, I advocate which you upload it in your commotion listing for conversation improvement. It is useful now not best for speak me and listening, however additionally for negotiating and main.

Maybe you have a friend, and you need to recognize if interested in you, its miles that you like and also you do no longer know the way to method him or her, or simply you meet her in a club and she/he looks interested by you, learn to examine her body language to recognize her emotions. You can see precisely what a thinks through analyzing her body language, be aware of the symptoms, study them, and use them for your advantage.

Make eye contact with the speaker so you can see his confidence when he is speaking to you.

Handshake: When shaking someone's hand, squeeze it three times hard to show confidence and happiness in the person you are meeting.

I mentioned that look is important, and numerous studies have supported this. People prefer to conduct business with those that look professional. Because how can you expect someone to take care of you if they do not take care of themselves?

Nobody will purchase food if his or her fingernails are dirty.

Smiling: Smiling is contagious, it relaxes your consumer, and it gives your voice a wonderful lively intonation.

Having good posture also conveys confidence in the speaker. It conveys a lot about your personality as well. Anything less, like slouching, makes you appear lazy and conveys to the other person in the connection that you don't believe in yourself and would rather be somewhere else, doing anything else.

According to studies, at least 7% of the messages you convey expressed through your sentences. 93% of the way there is nonverbal. The majority of communication—55%—is based on what people observe, while the remaining 38% is communicated through tone of voice. Consider it, then. People can see what you are not announcing in the business world. You are losing time if your body language does not correspond to your words.

The most obvious way to communicate is through eye contact. You exhibit your pastime when you're staring at the individual across from you. It conveys a lack of respect for the other person when you don't look them in the eye. On the approach to the appearance involved, maintain eye contact about 60% of the time, the way to appearance involved, however, not competitive.

The most obvious way to communicate is through eye contact. You exhibit your pastime when you are staring at the individual across from you. It conveys a lack of respect for the other person when you do not look them in the eye. On the approach to the appearance involved, maintain eye contact about 60% of the time,

Every other non-verbal communication method expressed through facial expression. Except in situations where it is literally a matter of life or death, a grin conveys a powerful message. A smile gives warmth and a sense of self-belief secrets. If you keep in mind to evaluate your expression, people may be more receptive.

Your mouth delivers several cues at other times besides simply while you are conversing.
Lips pursed or curled in one way, for example, can suggest that you are listening carefully or that you are trying to protect something.

Your head has a voice that humans can hear.
You will come across as assured and authoritative if you keep your head immediately, which is different from keeping your head on immediately.
People will be quite harsh with you.
If you want to come off as approachable and open, turn your head toward at least one of the aspects.

Your arm position communicates to others how receptive you are. Crossing your arms or folding them across your chest communicates that you have blocked out other people and have no interest in or what may be saying. This stance can also used to express disagreement. Even if you are bloodless, the person in front of you might think otherwise if you do not shiver simultaneously.

Your arm position communicates to others how receptive you are. Crossing your arms or folding them across your chest communicates that you have blocked out other people and have no interest in or what may be saying. This stance used to express disagreement. Even if you are bloodless, the person in front of you might think otherwise if you don't shiver simultaneously.

Additionally, how you move your arms might help or hurt your photo. To some, waving them roughly can also convey eagerness; to others, it conveys apprehension and immaturity. Your arms are the part of your body that is closest to them. The closest part of your body to your arms is by way of your side. You will appear assured and cozy. If that is hard for you, do what you consistently do when you want to get better at something: exercise. After some time, it will feel natural.

Additionally, how you move your arms might help or hurt your photo. To some, waving them roughly can also convey eagerness; to others, it conveys apprehension and immaturity. Your arms are the part of your body that is closest to them.

The angle of your body offers a demonstration to others approximately what is going on through your head.

Leaning in says, "Tell me more." Leaning away indicators, you have heard enough. Adding a nod of your head is every other manner to verify which you are listening.

Posture is just as important as your grandmother constantly said it changed into. Sit or stand erect if you need to seen as alert and enthusiastic. When you stop on chair, you look worn-out. No one wants to do enterprise with someone who has no power.

Control your arms by way of taking note of in which they are. In the enterprise international, particularly whilst you address human beings from different cultures, your palms need to seen. That might imply you ought to keep them from your pockets and you ought to withstand the urge to put them beneath the desk or in the back of you, returned. Having your arms anywhere above the neck, fidgeting together with your hair or rubbing your face, is unprofessional.

Legs speak, too. A lot of motion shows anxiousness. How and wherein you move them tells others how you experience. The preferred positions for the polished expert are toes flat on the floor or legs crossed on the ankles. The least professional and most offensive position is resting one leg or ankle on top of your different knee. Some people name this the "Figure Four." It could make you appearance conceited.

The distance you keep from others is essential in case you need to set up precise rapport. Standing too near or "in a person's face" will mark you as pushy. Positioning yourself to a ways away will make you seem standoffish. Neither is what you need so discover the happy medium. Most importantly, do what makes the other man or woman feel at ease. If the man or woman, with whom you are speaking, maintains backing far from you, stop. Either individual wishes space otherwise, you want a breath mint.

You may not be privy to what you are announcing together with your body, but others get the message.

Make certain it is the only you need to send.

Therefore, when your friend involves his body, his commitment level reaches the next level. So now, his or her relationship level reaches 66% commitment. Therefore, you can trust your relationship more.

GET BY MONEY RULE.

Your pals, family, and neighbours are all too keen to warn you of the pitfalls. I name it the "Get by Money

Rule". What is this, you ask? Well, in case you requested your friend for $2500.00 to pay the bills or for anything else. If pays for it. Its show that now they are more serious about relation. Once they made their mind to pay hard-earned money of the relationship. Always Here to Help a Friend in Need." They are satisfied that they can help you get there. All in all, being charitable makes people feel accurate. So does knowing they are in a better function than you are—it is a feeling of accomplishment for them and for you.

LOVE AND LOYALTY

Loyalty or fidelity manner dedicated, dedication that cannot damaged effortlessly. To be unswerving, approach to adhere to all of the promises made for the lifetime. To maintain all the commitments made for all time.

Loyalty is instead a completely easy word but a very laudable fine that is hard to maintain for loads many human beings.

Loyalty does now not bear in mind change in circumstances. If I am loyal to my associate and my associate meets with an coincidence that disfigures him/her badly, does now not mean that I depart to someone higher looking. If I commit to someone approximately my dating and that individual goes broke after someday, does now not imply that I will look for richer people. Every situation that comes tests loyalty. In a few nations the regulation permits you to break your marriage owes in case your accomplice goes lunatic. But many unswerving people do not break the relationship even at that time.

Every courting rests on believe and fact. If the relationship commenced with lies, it may never maintain.

The basis is of lies. How truth can grow from the seed of lie? The first need or requirement of getting into an extended-term dating is to be honest in all respects. Fooling others into believing untruths is a sin.

Once you've got decided to and committed loyalty, you must never wreck it under any instances. There can be no excuse for that. By doing such a act, we hurt the alternative partner

who believed in us, and we harm ourselves by using turning into an unfaithful and unreliable individual. We lose our shallowness totally after that. Once that occurs, the route is simplest downhill, all the way to hell. Love and loyalty cross collectively. How are we able to be disloyal in love? That is an not possible idea.

To love and cherished is a blessing. To wreck that via being disloyal is sinning towards goodness and God. If by means of any chance one does an act of disloyalty, one ought to right now confess and ask for forgiveness. Will the connection ever stay equal after this act of disloyalty? No. Unless one is fortunate to have an additional everyday accomplice, the connection will by no means remain the identical. Better to be a loyal and sincere individual always

CONCLUSION

Yes, it is the bitter but true truth. However, when money is entering, the person or a relation reaches the peak level. Because now we can say that the person is fully committed to his relationship, now we can say that the person, who is nearby, has been involved and committed at a level of 99%. Still, it is not 100%. As per human psychology, the mind does change according to condition and view. Still, we can say 99% is committed. I do have the value of time and relationships.

There are many ways to check the relationship.

- Crosscheck if your companion is telling the truth.
- When the timing is not favorable, how do your relations react? Reconsider your relationship.
- When time does not matter during conversation.
- Create small events to be memorable by cherishing each other.

Therefore, I would like to say that **heart, body,** and **money** are the parameters to check the commitment of a relationship. In other words, you can check the commitment level of others' relationships. Loyalty is a commitment to each other. In addition, commitment means quality and excellence.

Thanks for Reading.

Author: Rishi Pal Sharma